THE SPARK, THE FIRE, THE BLAZE

THE SPARK, THE FIRE, THE BLAZE

AWAKENING THE HEART OF THE CHURCH
A non-conventional interpretation of the Luke-Acts narrative

Mario Weyers

CWI
Christian World Imprints

First Published in 2019 by

Christian World Imprints
Christian Publishing & Books from India
H-12 Bali Nagar, **New Delhi-110015**
cwidelhi2017@gmail.com, info@christianworldimprints.com
www.ChristianWorldImprints.com
Phone: +91 11 25465925

ISBN: 978-93-5148-366-3

Printed in India.

CONTENTS

Introduction vii

Chapter 1: The Luke-Acts Narrative 1
The Socio-Historical Context 2
Chapter 2: The "Great Omission" 7
What Kind of Peace? 9
Chapter 3: Luke 12:49-53 as the Gateway to the Book of Acts 11
What Kind of a Rabbi? 12

Scripture is the Spark that Enables us to Respond to the Proclamation of Christ 13

Chapter 4: The Two Travellers to Emmaus 15
Setting Hearts on Fire 18
The Importance of Preaching and Teaching 19
A Text Book Jesus 21
Open Your Home (Heart) to Jesus 22
First Things First 22

The Holy Spirit is the Fire that Transforms us into the Likeness of the Risen Christ 25

Chapter 5: From Saviour to Master 27
From a Spark at Emmaus to a Fire in Jerusalem 28
What does this Mean? 29

	Prayer Kindle the Fire	31
	God not only with us but in us	34

Where The Church Submit to the Ongoing Preaching of Christ – A Blaze is Soon to Appear 37

Chapter 6:	The Heat Is On	39
	Submission of the Church to the Call of Christ	42
Chapter 7:	Critical Reflection	45
	Hospitality	47
Chapter 8:	How to Awaken the Heart of Your Church?	49
	Positioning for Authenticity Instead of Success	49
	The Church in Acts: An Ever Cathing-Up-With-God Kind of Church	50
	Envisioning Creativity and Innovation - Not Stagnation	52
	Beauty	53
	Acknowledge People – Not Programmes	55
	Individuality	56
Chapter 9:	Your Local Church Is God's New Creation	59
	What Ought to be Going on?	63

Appendix 65

Bibliography 67

INTRODUCTION

This book is my third contribution to ministry in Post Christendom society. My first publication, titled: *Belonging to the Church before believing in Christ* (Mediacom Education in Australia) was a response to the dilemma facing the Church in meeting the need of postmodern individuals to belong within the church, but not necessarily to practice believe. This is the ongoing issue of membership in the Church, in postmodern society, in a culture where consumerism and personal needs are prioritised above service and belief.

My second publication: *Your Church is God's New Creation* (Christian World Imprints-New Delhi) was to assist mainline historical congregations to reposition themselves for a positive future perspective on ministry in spite of a major Post Christendom paradigm.

The former publication dealt with the life of the Church on the inside of its meetings and ministry. Especially on how to relate to strangers and seekers wanting to join the Church with a non-Christian understanding or worldview. The latter was promoting a process to assist congregations in connecting with their specific community outside of its operational walls and to find new ways of expressing ministry in secular society.

This is my third response to the challenge of Post Christendom and is neither dealing with the inner or outer life of ministry of the Church, but in her ultimate calling and identity of making Christ known to a society that has become sceptical of the Church and its message of salvation. When mentioning the calling of the Church *in making Christ known* I refer to an evangelical response that appreciates the Biblical narrative in communicating within its familiar ecclesiastical boundaries as well as in Post Christendom society, with especially those that question Christianity's validity. An evangelical response, in making Christ known, have three specific criteria which I believe is also addressed in the Luke – Acts narrative:

- Scripture – that proclaims Christ.
- Spirit – that transforms us to the likeness of Christ.
- Submission (of the Church) – to the call of Christ.

The Church needs to (once again) *open her heart unreservedly to the Scriptures* that proclaim Christ, otherwise, she will have limited authority in proclaiming salvation in a Post Christendom context.

The Church needs to (once again) *open her heart in prayer* to the Holy Spirit that transforms us to the likeness of Christ, otherwise, she will not have the power to compete with the spirit of the new age.

The Church needs to (once again) *commit to the call of Christ* in sharing the message of salvation within a Post Christendom paradigm, otherwise, she will have a questionable foundation to build on.

This presentation, furthermore, is one that intends to give a Biblical foundation to the mandate of the Church to be a transformational institution, in not only meeting the needs of society (the Social gospel) but to affirm the power and purpose of its Founder, Jesus Christ. This is important because of the Post Christendom context that the Church operates in where society is sceptical of truth, rejects moral absolutes and proclaim that Christian belief is based on personal validation and not secured in Godly revelation.

In such a secular context an evangelical approach needs to be immersed in the *Biblical narrative, be Gospel centred and Christ-focused.*

I have chosen for a non-conventional approach to the *Luke-Acts* narrative. This approach could hardly be called a deconstruction, as it is practised in the discipline of philosophy, but do share a deconstructional aim in disturbing a conventional reading of the text in order to discover. By deconstructing a text, you learn to read beyond a text's straightforward content and uncover new meanings and truths.

In the words of Michael Horton[1]

> At the same time, many Reformed and Presbyterian churches seem content to live off of the capital of the past, without having to return for themselves to the streams that fed the great renewals of apostolic faith and practice in the past. We need to recover the fullness of biblical faith and practice in our own time and place. Like children, we need to ask even the most basic questions anew, in the light of the specific challenges and opportunities in our age.

May this study be such a fresh and liberating stream on the *Luke-Acts* narrative that it will encourage us to, once again, read this powerful biblical history on Jesus and his liberating message.

[1] Michael Horton, *For Calvinism* (Grand Rapids, Michigan: Zondervan, 2011).

Chapter 1

THE LUKE-ACTS NARRATIVE

Luke was a Gentile author that wrote for Christians who were mostly of Gentile origin. According to a short outline from Chuck Missler[2] is Luke's two-volume work not only the most complete narrative on the life of Jesus and the ministry of the early church but also the most authenticated historical writing in the New Testament. Luke has been considered to be a physician, a friend of Paul and even a painter.

Kirsten Abbott[3] explains that we can deduce a number of characteristics of Luke's written account: First, Luke's is a careful and orderly account, using several sources and witnesses. Second, Luke is explicit about the fact that he is constructing a narrative to convey the truth about Jesus to Theophilus (Theophilus was probably a man of wealth and social standing who converted to Christianity and could have sponsored Luke's writing initiative). Third, Luke-Acts is beautifully written, with far more skill than Mark's rough and ready

---

[2] Chuck Missler, *Learn the Bible in 24 hours* (Nashville: Thomas Nelson, 2002), 177

[3] Kirsten Abbott, "Themes in Luke's Gospel: Introduction to the Luke/Acts package." http://wn.anglican.org.nz/resources/links/teaching_helpful_links.

Greek. Fourth, Luke varies his style to suit different occasions (e.g. sometimes formal prose, sometimes Semitic idiom) and is finally proof of his ability to present his work in high standing to the public.

In this contribution, I shall support the general academic notion that Luke's intention was for the Luke-Acts narrative to be read back to back. The theme of the Holy Spirit (predominantly in the book of Acts) unites the time of Jesus and the time of the church in one era. Jesus and the church belong to one and the same era. Put slightly different: "The historical life of Jesus was not purely and simply relegated to the past. The church lives in continuity with the life and work of Jesus" (Bosch 1993:87).[4] This emerges clearly in the gospel of Luke, regarding Jesus ministry of good news and salvation, to be universal in intent but yet incomplete in execution until the powerful arrival of the Holy Spirit and the birth of the New Testament Church. The Gentile mission would be the responsibility of the coming church, not the historical Jesus.

Luke was concerned, at the time when he set out to write his two-volume work, for the church was facing both an identity crisis and an uncertain future. Some experts date the composition of the combined work to around 80–90 AD. This assumes that Acts was written after the Gospel of Luke (Acts 1:1). This also meant that more than half a century had passed since the momentous events took place surrounding the ministry, death and resurrection of Jesus of Nazareth.

THE SOCIO-HISTORICAL CONTEXT:

David Bosch[5] gives us insight into the socio-historical context that caused the missional crisis at hand:

> The Christian church, which began as a renewal movement within Judaism had, during the preceding four decades or so, undergone an almost complete transformation. It was no longer winning any significant numbers of Jews to faith

[4] David J. Bosch, *Transforming Mission* (Maryknoll, New York: Orbis Books, 1993), 87

[5] David J. Bosch, *Transforming Mission* (Maryknoll, New York: Orbis Books, 1993), 85

in Jesus Christ. It had, in fact, for all intents and purposes become a Gentile church.

Needless to say that the missionary enterprise of Paul was responsible for the mostly Gentile character and profile of the church at around 80 AD. Unfortunately, by then, was the heyday of Paul's missionary expansion part of a pioneering past as a degree of stagnation had set in.

David Bosch[6] mentions six reasons for the stagnation and loss of ministry focus:

- The church was now a church of the second generation and did not function as an early movement with the excitement and dedication of participants like in the past.
- The return of Christ, as expected by the first generation, did not take place. Expectation made way for routine.
- From within, the faith of the participants in the church was losing enthusiasm.
- From without, there were hostility and opposition from both Jews and Gentiles.
- Gentile Christians were facing an identity crisis in regard to their religion being either a continuation of Judaism or a new reality made possible by the post-resurrection events?
- Above all, they were uncertain how to relate to the earthly Jesus who was receding into the past.

Luke decided to write his two-volume work to assist the church during its difficult transitional phase. The salvation history of half a century could not simply be passed over but needed to be reinterpreted. Luke would remind his readers that the risen Lord was still among them, particularly through his Spirit. Believers in the community had to be reminded to trust on the name of the Lord and be efficacious in his power. The faith community could indeed follow the lead of the Spirit into a new paradigm of their mission.

---

[6] Ibid

All of the above six criteria corresponds remarkably well with the current Post-Christian challenges that face the Church today: secularism, liberalism, atheism, agnosticism and socialism to mention only a few. These powers in society are not only well and alive but creates an environment where the Church does feel at times to have lost its direction, purpose and sense of calling amidst many other voices and trends.

Thomas Schreiner[7] explains in his commentary on Luke that the author (Luke) did indeed help his fellow believers reinterpret their future faith journey from at least four fresh perspectives:

- *To assure his readers of the certainty of what they have been taught.* That the events recorded in the Luke-Acts material were not by chance but were the fulfilment of ancient prophecy. Therefore it carried authority.
- *To help his readers understand how Israel's rejection of Jesus and the Gentiles did not derail God's divine plan.* That Christianity, in general, and the witnessing church in particular, growing conflict with worldly powers and entities does not keep the Holy Spirit from accomplishing the task at hand.
- *To clarify for his readers Jesus' teaching concerning the end times.* Jesus did not teach that the Parousia (Return of Christ) would come *soon* but that the Holy Spirit would become the substitute. In this way, Luke solved the problem caused by the delay of the Parousia (cf. Bosch 1993:86).[8]
- *To emphasize that his readers need not to fear Rome.* The Church engulfed by power struggles with strong worldly forces do need to focus on the post-resurrection witnesses Lk. 24:1-51 (NIV), proclaiming Jesus to be alive and journeying with his people as he promised.

---

[7] Thomas R. Schreiner, ed., *ESV Study Bible: Luke (*Wheaton: Crossway, 2008), 1935.

[8] David J. Bosch, *Transforming Mission* (Maryknoll, New York: Orbis Books, 1993), 86

Luke decided to come to the aid of the Christian community who needed to anticipate God's future for them in a new way. Luke understood the challenge created by the passage of time and of the transformation of the Christian community from being exclusively Jewish to being predominantly Gentile.

Chapter 2

THE "GREAT OMISSION"[9]

We are well acquainted with Matthew 28: 18-20 (NIV) to be the classical missionary text in the New Testament:

> [18] Then Jesus came to them and said, "All authority in heaven and on earth has been given to me. [19] Therefore go and make disciples of all nations, baptizing them in the name of the Father and of the Son and of the Holy Spirit, [20] and teaching them to obey everything I have commanded you. And surely I am with you always, to the very end of the age."

Here we find the commission used in the imperative sense: *matheteusate,* "to go and make disciples." The two subordinate actions are "baptizing" and "teaching" and describe how to go about making disciples for the Kingdom of God.

---

[9] I have named this chapter after the book written by Dallas Willard with the same heading.

In the Gospel of Luke chapter 24:46-49 (NIV) we find a similar calling of the disciples to reach the nations with the message of salvation:

> [46] He told them, "This is what is written: The Messiah will suffer and rise from the dead on the third day, [47] and repentance for the forgiveness of sins will be preached in his name to all nations, beginning at Jerusalem.[48] You are witnesses of these things. [49] I am going to send you what my Father has promised; but stay in the city until you have been clothed with power from on high."

The above is considered to be Luke's entire understanding of the Christian mission: its central theme is the salvation message intended for "all nations" and is to be executed by "witnesses" in the power of the Holy Spirit. These elements argue Bosch (1993:91)[10]: "constitute the fibres of Luke's mission theology running through both the Gospel and Acts, binding this two-volume work together." It is generally accepted, like in the case with Matthew's gospel, that Luke's missiology should by default be appreciated and primarily understood from the perspective of the final periscope (24:36-53). With introducing a new perspective on Luke 12:49-53 I want to differ with the above statement in claiming that to understand the *missiological* connection between the Gospel of Luke and the Acts of the Apostles it is not so much the final periscope, but the central periscope (Luke 12:49-53) that reveals Luke's mission theology.

There is, therefore, another way to interpret the missional link between Luke's gospel and the Acts of the Apostles. Luke 12:49-53 is another key text, I believe, to connect the Gospel of Luke with the content in Acts. This, above mentioned perspective has not been considered in the past. This is why I refer to Luke 12:49-53 as the: *"great omission."* The following is written in Luke 12:49-53 (NIV):

> [49] "I have come to bring fire on the earth, and how I wish it were already kindled! [50] But I have a baptism to undergo, and what constraint I am under until it is completed! [51] Do

[10] David J. Bosch, *Transforming Mission* (Maryknoll, New York: Orbis Books, 1993), 91

> you think I came to bring peace on earth? No, I tell you,
> but division. [52] From now on there will be five in one
> family divided against each other, three against two and
> two against three. [53] They will be divided, father against
> son and son against father, mother against daughter and
> daughter against mother, mother-in-law against daughter-in-law and daughter-in-law against mother-in-law."

We all shall agree that this above mentioned scripture is no explicit commissioning of the Church, as in a traditional reading that we would find in the case of Matthew 28: 18-20 or Luke 24:46-49, but is rich with intrinsic missiological implications that will become clear as we, later on, investigate how Luke 12:49-53 becomes key in reading Luke 24 through to Acts: 2:47.

In the above reading, we find, as often was the case with Jesus teaching, him using shocking overstatements to convey a truth that he needs his followers to grasp at all cost. This strategy from Jesus, make Luke 12:49-53 to be of key importance in reading the rest of the narrative.

WHAT KIND OF PEACE?

Jesus cannot wait for the final stage of his mission to come alive – the fire of the Holy Spirit to be released after the post-resurrection events. *Anapto* from *ana* implies the start or up-rising of fire and *hapto* means to "light up" and comes from the fact that it was through fastening and rubbing things together that fire was produced. *Kindle* means to cause something to begin to burn or catch fire, to set on fire; to ignite. This was to occur after Jesus faced the judgement of his Father. Jesus would soon become the One that would carry the burden and punishment for the sins of humanity. Therefore we find Jesus under stress in awaiting his own suffering and crucifixion.

Though his message is a different kind of peace, it is such a hard-won peace that it is more like division because not all would understand its context, motivation or blessing. Jesus knows that the radical content of his message will cause people to waiver and doubt and oppose his message. He is like the prophet Micah, whom Luke quotes here, who, while seeing the divisions in families, puts his trust in God alone (Micah 7:6-7).

Jesus is warning his disciples that, after he has gone, they could expect antagonism and confrontation in their future identification with his mission. They would be hauled before rulers and governors, they would be beaten and jailed and put to death. People would think they were doing well in ridding the world of them. In that sense, Jesus was certainly not going to bring peace.

Jesus himself would also not be dismissed from being wrongly understood, badly labelled and cursed to eventually die on a Roman cross. The reference to *baptism* in the above scripture refers to Jesus immersion in the terrible suffering and death that awaits him. In fact, the ritual of baptism where the person to be baptised was immersed in the baptismal pool was seen as a parallel to Jesus going down into death and emerging to the new life of the resurrection.

Only after such suffering and death, resurrection awaits, with the final stage of Jesus mission to take place: the commissioning of his disciples as they trust on the promise of a life- empowering experience.

Chapter 3

LUKE 12:49-53 AS THE GATEWAY TO THE BOOK OF ACTS

It is striking that Luke 12:49-53 is the centre text or scripture portion outlined, in regards to the complete written gospel of Luke, which ends with chapter 24:53. I am not promoting something mystical in making such a statement apart from acknowledging that from chapter 12 onwards Jesus teaching intensifies as he sets out on his final journey towards Jerusalem where his hearing, death and resurrection awaits. Luke 12:49-53 is therefore not only the most "central" portion of teaching but also crucial in connecting the Gospel of Luke with the Acts of the Apostles.

What follows, in the following chapters, are a description of how Luke 12:49-53 functions as a door hinge that opens' a gateway between Luke's Gospel on the one hand and his description on the birth and progress of the early church in the book of Acts, on the other. I do believe that Luke 12:49-53 is a key text in reading and understanding Luke 24:1 through to Acts 2:47.

WHAT KIND OF A RABBI?

Luke, among other objectives, want's to reveal *who Jesus is* to his contemporaries who did not understand how to relate to the historical Jesus. He wanted to help them anticipate what a future with God and the church could hold. Therefore do we find, in the Gospel of Luke, at least four occasions where the question are presented in regards to *who Jesus is*? Verses *5:21, 7:49, 8:25* and *9:9* confirm this motive. The following responses follow:

- Jesus is the Messiah (9:20).
- Jesus is the One that will bring fire (Judgement) on the earth (12:49).
- Jesus is the Saviour of the world (19:10).
- Jesus is Lord (20:44).

My emphasis in this presentation on *who Jesus is* and what he would do, after the post-resurrection events, is based on the second answer above. That Jesus would be the One that would cause severe and conflicting consequences for both believers and non-believers that would affect the future of the Church yet to be established. In short: Jesus would soon be the cause of a *spark,* which would kindle a *fire* to set *ablaze* events that would forever set the Church apart from any other organisation or human invention.

SCRIPTURE IS THE
SPARK THAT ENABLES
US TO RESPOND TO THE
PROCLAIMATION OF CHRIST

Chapter 4

THE TWO TRAVELLERS TO EMMAUS

Luke 24:13-35 New International Version (NIV)

13 Now that same day two of them were going to a village called Emmaus, about seven miles[a] from Jerusalem. **14** They were talking with each other about everything that had happened. **15** As they talked and discussed these things with each other, Jesus himself came up and walked along with them; **16** but they were kept from recognizing him.

17 He asked them, "What are you discussing together as you walk along?"

They stood still, their faces downcast. **18** One of them, named Cleopas, asked him, "Are you the only one visiting Jerusalem who does not know the things that have happened there in these days?"

19 "What things?" he asked.

"About Jesus of Nazareth," they replied. "He was a prophet, powerful in word and deed before God and all the people. **20** The chief priests and our rulers handed him over to be sentenced to death, and they crucified him; **21** but we had hoped that he was the one who was going to redeem Israel. And what is more, it is the third day since all this took place. **22** In addition, some of our women amazed us. They went to the tomb early this morning **23** but didn't find his body. They came and told us that they had seen a vision of angels, who said he was alive. **24** Then some of our companions went to the tomb and found it just as the women had said, but they did not see Jesus."

25 He said to them, "How foolish you are, and how slow to believe all that the prophets have spoken! 26 Did not the Messiah have to suffer these things and then enter his glory?" **27** And beginning with Moses and all the Prophets, he explained to them what was said in all the Scriptures concerning himself.

28 As they approached the village to which they were going, Jesus continued on as if he were going farther. **29** But they urged him strongly, "Stay with us, for it is nearly evening; the day is almost over." So he went in to stay with them.

30 When he was at the table with them, he took bread, gave thanks, broke it and began to give it to them. **31** Then their eyes were opened and they recognized him, and he disappeared from their sight. **32** They asked each other, "Were not our hearts burning within us while he talked with us on the road and opened the Scriptures to us?"

33 They got up and returned at once to Jerusalem. There they found the Eleven and those with them, assembled together **34** and saying, "It is true! The Lord has risen and has appeared to Simon." **35** Then the two told what had happened on the way, and how Jesus was recognized by them when he broke the bread.

One of the two Emmaus travellers, travelling to their destination, was called Cleopas. This could have been a husband travelling with his wife. They were going to Emmaus possibly after having celebrated the Passover in Jerusalem. The precise location of Emmaus is uncertain, but it was in Judea approximately 11 km from Jerusalem.

Towards the end of the Gospel of Luke the two travellers to Emmaus express their desire and hope that Jesus was the one to redeem Israel (24:21). Similarly, at the beginning of Acts (1:6) the disciples ask the risen Lord: "Lord, will you at this time restore the kingdom to Israel?" The disciples are talking about the same hope as the travellers to Emmaus. Jesus respond to the two travellers in a way that connects his current death and resurrection not only with the words of the prophets (Luke 24:25-26), but also his own words as once spoken off in Luke 12:49-50: "*I have come to bring fire on the earth, and how I wish it were already kindled! But I have a baptism to undergo, and what constraint I am under until it is completed.*" The entire Old Testament had shown how God brought his chosen vessels first through suffering and then to glory. In fulfilment of this extensive pattern and in fulfilment of many prophecies, would also the Messiah first suffer before entering into his promised glory.

As Jesus was bringing insight to these two travellers in the events of the past few days, they urged Jesus to stay with them for the night. What follows is best described by looking into Jewish custom:[11]

In the Babylonian Talmud, we read: "The host should break bread" (Berakoth 46). In Jewish tradition, the host – the head of the household – is the one who always says the blessing and breaks the bread. Strangers who are invited to the meal usually wait for directions from their host and quietly receive what is set before them.

However, that is not the case here. Because this was not a regular guest! Instead of waiting for his host's direction, this stranger is taking the host's place: He is saying the blessing and breaking the bread! This is indeed out of the ordinary. We can imagine that this behaviour must have caught the attention of everyone in the house. Where did this authority come from?

Scholars explain that the Qumran Sectarians seemed to believe in the eternal Saviour (they believed it was Melchizedek), who would come as man and was known to them as the Teacher of Righteousness. The Teacher of Righteousness was a priest. Let us have a look on a fragmentary document 1QSa (sometimes called *The Messianic Rule*) and see what this text says about the Priest; *[the Messiah of Israel shall*

[11] www.http//eTeacher Biblical – Israel Academy of Language and History

[enter] … and [no-one should stretch out] his hand to the first fruit … before the Priest, for [he is the one who blesses the first-fruit of the bread and of the new wine … … (column 2, lines 18-21).

'No-one should stretch out his hand to bless the bread'**:** it means that, in the days of Jesus public ministry, there was an understanding that when the Messiah came, no-one should stretch out his hand to bless the bread before Him. The authority to bless the bread first clearly belonged to the host – or to the Messiah. And when, in the above story, this stranger acted in the house as *one that had authority,* we can imagine that, even though the eyes of the couple were still restrained, their hearts that had been burning along the way were now filled with excitement and anticipation. Jesus behaviour was a definite sign to them of His messianic personality.

SETTING HEARTS ON FIRE:

As soon as the two travellers to Emmaus caught on to who it was that was sharing their journey and the evening meal with them that their hearts were set on fire: Καρδια ημων καιομενη… (Luke 24:32). **"Were not our hearts burning within us?"** What Jesus predicted he would do according to Luke 12: 49 after his suffering and death, in bringing fire, has just started. On realising that their guest, who was no other than the resurrected Lord, had not only energised them in returning to Jerusalem at night but have given them a mission and a mandate to share this amazing news - spurred on by a burning internal flame! This event is best described by Roland Allen (1962:5)[12] when he remarks:

> St Luke fixes our attention, not upon an external voice, but upon an internal Spirit. This manner of command is peculiar to the Gospel. Others direct from without, Christ directs within; others order, Christ inspires…This is the manner of the command in St Luke's writings. He speaks not of men who, being what they were, strove to obey the last orders of a beloved Master, but of men who, receiving a

---

[12] Allen Roland, *Missionary Methods: St. Pauls or Ours?* (London: Dominion Press 1962), 5

Spirit, were driven by that Spirit to act in accordance with the nature of that Spirit.

In Luke 24:13-53 we find two technicalities that are of importance for this chapter. According to Luke 12:35 the two Emmaus travellers acknowledged that they recognised Jesus when he broke the bread. That was when the penny dropped. This was the moment that the glorified Christ was revealed to them: "Then the two told what had happened on the way, and how Jesus was recognized by them when he broke the bread."

But the spark that ignited the reality and truth of the post-resurrection events in their hearts, were the portions of Scripture that Jesus shared with them on their journey (24:27 and 24:32):[13]

"And beginning with Moses and all the Prophets, he explained to them what was said in all the Scriptures concerning himself."

"They asked each other, "Were not our hearts burning within us while he talked with us on the road and opened the Scriptures to us?"

THE IMPORTANCE OF PREACHING AND TEACHING:[14]

Knowledge of Christianity and Christ's saving mediation is rather limited among Post-Christian communities which do not have a historic bond with the Christendom era. Post-Christian seekers and those interested in what Christianity teaches need to hear the Gospel and its wider content numerous times. Why? Because Christian culture seems strange to the current and upcoming generation who is not familiar with the content of the Bible, the Gospel narrative or Christian jargon as practised inside the context of a congregation. Teaching the content of the Bible, preaching to those who are eager to listen and releasing biblical principles are what I believe to be the primary work of the Church in a Post Christendom culture as communities become more secularised and individuals' life's more fragmented.

---

[13] See also Luke 24:44-45.

[14] Mario Weyers, *From minutes that matter to sermons that surprise* (New-Delhi: Christian World Imprints, 2019), x-xii

In the past, Western culture was influenced and shaped by an overall Biblical worldview. With the arrival of the Enlightenment or the Age of Reason (1685-1815), the Church started competing with other voices. Many of these other voices (science and philosophy) were mostly in direct opposition to what the Church through the ages proclaimed and preached. Today these other voices seem to be the dominant ones' as the dissonance between faith and reason are on the increase.

Therefore, we need a clear Christological principle in our preaching and teaching – which means that Scripture is to be interpreted in light of God's central revelation in Jesus Christ.

The *Christological principle* for me is an evangelical one. You cannot preach on the person or ministry of Christ and the realisation of His kingdom without elaborating on Jesus role as the Anointed One who was sent to die for the sins of the world. Preaching on Christ is nothing less than the inherent message of Good news, for Christ and the cross are inseparable. Preaching on Christ is by implication the intrinsic proclamation of the gospel, for Jesus is the central revelation of God's love. Romans 1:16 states:

"For I am not ashamed of the gospel, because it is the power of God that brings salvation to everyone who believes: first to the Jew, then to the Gentile."

Furthermore, I want to stress, not only the importance in presenting Scripture in a Post-Christian context in comparing Old Testament Scripture with Old Testament Scripture or New Testament Scripture with New Testament Scripture but inter-relating the Old and New in interpreting God's word for today. This is particularly important when preparing conversations and presentations to postmodern communities who, from lack of understanding, consider Scripture to be fragmented, inconsistent and at its worse a paradox.

When preaching sermons or clarifying the Scriptures that do relate to both the Old and New Testament (as in the New Testament confirming or elaborating on Scripture in the Old Testament or The Old Testament being brought to completion in the New Testament) one not only promotes the unity and inter-connectedness of Scripture but targets the general misconception that the Bible contradicts itself. For many postmodern individuals it can be surprising to find that the Bible is mostly holistic in its presentation of the Gospel and, to be more precise, that the Old Testament is brought to light only when reading it through the scope of the New. Understanding that the Old- and New Testament are closely connected and revealing that in our preaching, is what I believe brings the word of God to life.

May we not consider preaching to be important in producing growing numbers or gratitude towards us in our churches, but to make Jesus Christ the main act on centre stage with the Old and New Testament as powerful stage lights clearly alighting the birth, ministry, death and resurrection of Jesus Christ.

A TEXT BOOK JESUS:

In Luke chapter 24 we find Jesus presenting a *contextual* and *conversational* approach. A contextual and conversational approach is key when addressing Post-Christian communities. Jesus seem to be approaching the two travellers to Emmaus as if he has just graduated from Bible school with Cum Laude!

- Jesus approach was relational and respectful (Luke 24:15-16).
- Jesus revealed interest and enquired into their situation. Prioritising people before programmes (Luke 24:17).
- Jesus used strategic questions in order to win people and not arguments (Luke 24:19).
- Jesus stuck to being relational in his response and not doctrinal (Luke 24:27) which gave him the opportunity to be invited, as a guest, into the home of the Emmaus travellers (Luke 24:28-29).

As a missiologist, I cannot find any fault to penalise the Lukean' Jesus in his approach. It is simply flawless. But the essential part of this story is what happened when Jesus entered the home of the two travellers on their invitation.

OPEN YOUR HOME (HEART) TO JESUS:

For the Emmaus couple to have their lives transformed by the teaching of Jesus, to have him spark their spirit and light a fire in their heart they had to invite him into their home. They had to open up their private living space even if he was to them a stranger that they have known for only the duration of their journey...a fellow traveller.

A transformational experience is possible when recipients of the gospel message open their lives (heart) to receive the risen son of God take residents in their life.

In Jesus journey with the Emmaus travellers, we find a striking resemblance with Revelation 3:20

"Here I am! I stand at the door and knock. If anyone hears my voice and opens the door, I will come in and eat with that person, and they with me."

The church in Laodicea needed transformation as she were neither cold nor hot. She is described as being lukewarm (χλιαρος). The use of this word in this context can be translated as being unenthusiastic...to have lost one's fire and excitement for a cause. The congregation in Laodicea has clearly lost their fire and passion for the gospel of Jesus Christ and had been consumed with consumerism and the good life.

The remedy for the church in Laodicea, as well as for the depressed and unenthusiastic two travellers to Emmaus, to regain their passion and to receive the spark that would light their spiritual life would be to open their "home" (their hearts) to Jesus Christ. When Jesus enters our life, with the intent to spark his presence in our innermost being, we have the privilege of experiencing authentic fellowship with him as portrait in both passages by sharing in a meal.

FIRST THINGS FIRST:

Luke 24:36-45 New International Version (NIV):

36 While they were still talking about this, Jesus himself stood among them and said to them, "Peace be with you."

37 They were startled and frightened, thinking they saw a
ghost. **38** He said to them, "Why are you troubled, and why do

doubts rise in your minds? [39] Look at my hands and my feet. It is I myself! Touch me and see; a ghost does not have flesh and bones, as you see I have."

40 When he had said this, he showed them his hands and feet. **41** And
while they still did not believe it because of joy and amazement, he asked them, "Do you have anything here to eat?" **42** They gave him
a piece of broiled fish, **43** and he took it and ate it in their presence.

44 He said to them, "This is what I told you while I was still with you: Everything must be fulfilled that is written about me in the Law of Moses, the Prophets and the Psalms."

45 Then he opened their minds so they could understand the Scriptures.

In Luke 24:36 we find that the Emmaus travellers have by now reached Jerusalem again and are sharing their new found joy with the remaining 11 disciples. In the meantime, Jesus arrives on the scene and joins the meeting to confirm, in a very physical way, the testimony of the two Emmaus travellers. Then we find in Luke 24:45 this striking statement that Jesus opened the minds (νουν) of all thirteen at the gathering (two from Emmaus + eleven disciples from Jerusalem) so they could understand the Scriptures.[15] In the previous periscope, it was the two Emmaus' travellers that opened their home to Jesus, because Jesus previously had set off a spark in their heart (καρδια) in sharing scriptural witnesses on the death and resurrection of the Messiah. Now in joining the other eleven disciples it is Jesus bringing insight and perspective not to their hearts, but their minds.

First Jesus propels our *heart* towards him in setting off a spiritual spark in our inner being and then later he transforms our *mind.* What is significant about this? It seems like two separate processes. When we initially open our heart (our most inner being with all its unique personality traits) to Jesus it does not imply that our mind (intellectual understanding) is, at the onset, on the same frequency level in fully comprehending the kingdom of God. We do not need

[15] See Acts 16:14

to understand God or all of Scripture before fully committing our future life to Christ. In due time Jesus will open our intellect and understanding to all that is necessary for us to grasp the risen Lord in all his faculties. We, above all, need to respond to the spark, for without it we will miss out on the fire.

In Luke 24:13-53 we witnessed the reality of the key words spoken by Jesus in Luke 12:49 which states: "I have come to bring fire on the earth, and how I wish it were already kindled!" The spark was executed now it was time for the fire to ignite!

THE HOLY SPIRIT IS THE FIRE THAT TRANSFORMS US INTO THE LIKENESS OF THE RISEN CHRIST

Chapter 5

FROM SAVIOUR TO MASTER

Where the *Gospel of Luke* (and especially Luke 24:1-53) reveal and confirm that Jesus Christ is indeed the promised Messiah, the Anointed One that was sent to save the lost, we find that the *Acts of the Apostles* puts the emphasis on the Holy Spirit as Master of the Church. Directing, protecting and providing for those coming to faith in Christ, even more so in regards to those obeying the voice and intervention of the Holy Spirit.

Luke, as the author of the Gospel, accentuated the importance of knowing Jesus as the promised Saviour who was sent to redeem us from our sin and transgressions. Luke, as the author of Acts, highlighted the importance of acknowledging the Master-ship of the Holy Spirit. It was indeed through the Spirit that the risen Christ was powerfully present in every community that the apostles ministered in. Rightly so that many refer to the *Acts of the Apostles* as the "Acts of the Holy Spirit" (cf. Acts 11:12, 13:1-3, 16:6-10). In Mark and Matthew, the Spirit is not as prominent as in Luke's writings. Among the evangelists he may be singled out as the "theologian of the Holy Spirit"[16] as David Bosch[17] explains:

> Luke realized that Jesus' mission and ministry had to be reinterpreted for the church of his own time, and he believed that this reinterpretation would be mediated by the Spirit. He did not introduce this notion only at Pentecost. The ministry of the earthly Jesus is already portrayed in terms of the initiative and guidance of the Spirit.

FROM A SPARK AT EMMAUS TO A FIRE IN JERUSALEM:

The two Emmaus travellers have sparked excitement and most probably even fear among the eleven disciples when they returned to Jerusalem to share the news that Jesus was truly alive (Luke 24:35). According to Luke, Jesus foretold his suffering and death to the disciples at least three times (Luke 9:22, 9:44 and 18:31), but only now do we find that the post-resurrection events are slowly but surely hitting home. As a confirmation, Jesus himself appears in the gathering to reveal his living presence to them (Luke 24:36).

Jesus not only appeared in person to convince the disciples that he had risen according to the Scriptures (Luke 24:45), but to reveal to them and prepare them for the supernatural manifestation of the Holy Spirit:

"I am going to send you what my Father has promised; but stay in the city until you have been clothed with power from on high" (Luke 24:49).

For any spark to cause a serious fire you need wind or a fuelling source to ignite a flame into a burning fire. Jesus was about to set exactly that in motion as we now continue with this future dramatic event as forecast in Luke 12:49 and described by Luke in Acts 2:1-12.

Acts 2:1-12 New International Version (NIV)

---

[16] David J. Bosch, *Transforming Mission* (Maryknoll, New York: Orbis Books, 1993), 113.

[17] Ibid

1 When the day of Pentecost came, they were all together in one place.
2 suddenly a sound like the blowing of a violent wind came from
heaven and filled the whole house where they were sitting. **3** They
saw what seemed to be tongues of fire that separated and came to rest
on each of them. **4** All of them were filled with the Holy Spirit and
began to speak in other tongues as the Spirit enabled them.

5 Now there were staying in Jerusalem God-fearing Jews from
every nation under heaven. **6** When they heard this sound, a crowd
came together in bewilderment, because each one heard their own
language being spoken. **7** Utterly amazed, they asked: "Aren't all
these who are speaking Galileans? **8** Then how is it that each of us
hears them in our native language? **9** Parthians, Medes and Elamites;
residents of Mesopotamia, Judea and Cappadocia, Pontus and
Asia, **10** Phrygia and Pamphylia, Egypt and the parts of Libya near
Cyrene; visitors from Rome**11** (both Jews and converts to Judaism);
Cretans and Arabs—we hear them declaring the wonders of God
in our own tongues!" **12** Amazed and perplexed, they asked one
another, "What does this mean?"

WHAT DOES THIS MEAN?

The question remains: *What does this mean?*[18] The underlining purpose of Pentecost was not to make the church more supernaturally "Pentecostal" but to move the church to be speaking participants in "declaring the wonders of God!" The small faith community was fuelled into flame with the purpose of being witnesses. The Church is in crisis when the world does not hear us speak and witness about the great works of God: Salvation to all in the name of Jesus Christ. Therefore, was the Holy Spirit given to the church to empower the former fearful disciples with burning courage and boldness in going forth with the message of salvation.

[18] The Holy Spirit was not given primarily as a revelation of God's power as it was meant to be an encouraging revelation of God's PRESENCE, filling the emptiness that was left with Jesus ascension. Not to make the church more Pentecostal, but more OBEDIENT in setting up the church in Jerusalem to become a PLATFORM from where the Spirit could now operate God's global mission.

Ever since the early church fathers, commentators have seen the blessing of Pentecost as a deliberate and dramatic reversal of the curse of Babel.[19] It is important to note that the division of languages originates with God at Babel and that the healing of that division began with the gift of the Holy Spirit to the church at Pentecost: "Yet we see that the unity or singularity that was there from creation, lost at the fall and scattered at Babel was then restored at Pentecost, in answer to Christ's prayers in John 17 (17:21, 'may be one'; verse 22, 'one as we are one'; verse 23, 'complete unity')."[20]

Mankind is seen in Genesis 11 organizing and aligning to himself essentially divine prerogatives: he builds a tower to reach God's dwelling in heaven and he tries to make himself a name in spite of obeying God's command to fill the Earth (Genesis 1:28, 9:1,7). So, at Babel, God divides language into all the resulting tongues of the world, in the last judgment of primeval times.

Babylonians believed that Babel/Babylon meant 'gate of God', from the Akkadian language.[21] Thus, it was the gate by means of which humans sought to compete with God. Babel was meant to be the high point of culture but has rather became the symbol of human defiance and failure. A secondary motif in this project, in building the tower, was not exclusively to only storm the gates of heaven but to be a central point of reference that could be seen by all; it was not to serve as simply a literal pointer back to the centre of civilisation but to figuratively keep civilisation evolving.

The Pneumatological promise of fire and its subsequent boldness to speak, that is related to Acts 1:8, was fulfilled when the Holy Spirit came upon the 120 disciples gathered in the upper room on the day of Pentecost (50 days after the Passover). The Holy Spirit not only gifts the disciples to speak with 'tongues' but also empowers them to perform 'signs and wonders' in the name of Jesus Christ.

---

[19] Alexander Soal and Desmond Henry. The Reversal of Babel: Questioning the early Church's understanding of the gift of the Holy Spirit in Acts as a reversal of the curse of Babel. *Verbum et Ecclesia, vol. 39, no.1 (2018).*

[20] Ibid

[21] Ibid

As the disciples gathered for what was originally the religious festival of first-fruits of the wheat harvest, the Holy Spirit came on them as the wind (πνοῆς) and with 'tongues' (γλῶσσαι) as of fire (πυρός). The analogy of the tongues of fire (Acts 2:3) most probably points forward to the 'tongues' of spoken languages in Acts 2:4. The Holy Spirit had been associated earlier with fire by John the Baptist (Luke 3:16). The tongues of fire were distributed [διαμεριζόμεναι] upon each disciple, just as the Holy Spirit had descended upon Christ Jesus in the form of a dove according to John 1:32. In the same manner that Jesus was acknowledged and empowered in the event that the Holy spirit descended upon him, the disciples are acknowledged as apostles and empowered to be God's future messengers. In sending the Holy Spirit to the disciples in Jerusalem, a fire was released that not only set their mouths alight to proclaim the wonders of God but changed them forever into Apostles (sent ones) preaching salvation unto the ends of the earth.

Luke, as the likely author of both the Gospel of Luke and Acts, has taken care throughout both books to establish a continuous link between God's actions in the past with Israel and his actions in the making of the church. For this reason, it is probable that Luke deliberately constructed the Pentecost account in Acts 2 as a counter-balance to the Babel story in Genesis 11.

This leads to the conclusion that the primary purpose of the gift of tongues was not intended to start a controversial debate in regards to modern day glossolalia but rather focus on the supernatural revelation of the Holy Spirit in equipping the Apostles to be with power and potential in moving unreservedly into the known world with a Godly message, spoken in a recognisable language, that has been ignited by heaven itself. They were mobilised with a universal message which not only had the potential to be understood by all but to start a blaze.

PRAYER KINDLE THE FIRE:

Anapto is written in the *aorist passive* voice (*kindled being ignited*), which implies that it is an event that is strictly speaking not initiated by human engineering but a given that we may witness as happening to us. This becomes apparently clear when we read the following from Acts 1:4-5

> [4] "On one occasion, while he was eating with them, he gave them this command: 'Do not leave Jerusalem, but wait for the gift my Father promised, which you have heard me speak about. [5] For John baptized with water, but in a few days you will be baptized with the Holy Spirit.' "

This instruction- *to wait*- περιμενειν is written in the *present active* tense. To wait on the promise of the Holy Spirit in a manner regardless of any obstacles involved. Although the expected fire is not humanly engineered and needs to be waited upon with a sense of expectation and seriousness, it does not imply being totally inactive or simply doing nothing. Luke tells us that after Jesus was taken up into heaven, the apostles returned to Jerusalem to an upper room where they were staying and joined together constantly in prayer along with the women (Luke 1:14). They could not manufacture the coming and blessing of the Holy Spirit, but they would actively contribute in prayer for the Holy Spirit to come and fill the emptiness that occurred with Jesus departure.

We have evidence in Scripture (Old and New Testament) that confirms that God sent fire from heaven when asked in prayer. 1 Kings 18:16-46 tells the story of Elijah challenging the Baal prophets on Mount Carmel:

1 Kings 18:30-39 New International Version (NIV)

30 Then Elijah said to all the people, "Come here to me." They came to him, and he repaired the altar of the LORD, WHICH HAD BEEN TORN DOWN.**31** Elijah took twelve stones, one for each of the tribes descended from Jacob, to whom the word of the LORD HAD COME, SAYING, "YOUR NAME SHALL BE ISRAEL." **32** With the stones he built an altar in the name of the LORD, AND HE DUG A TRENCH AROUND IT LARGE ENOUGH TO HOLD TWO SEAHS (7.3 LITRES) OF SEED. **33** He arranged the wood, cut the bull into pieces and laid it on the wood. Then he said to them, "Fill four large jars with water and pour it on the offering and on the wood."

34 "Do it again," he said, and they did it again.

"Do it a third time," he ordered, and they did it the third time. **35** The water ran down around the altar and even filled the trench.

36 At the time of sacrifice, the prophet Elijah stepped forward and prayed: "LORD, the God of Abraham, Isaac and Israel, let it be known today that you are God in Israel and that I am your servant and have done all these things at your command. **37** Answer me, LORD, answer me, so these people will know that you, Lord, are God, and that you are turning their hearts back again."

38 Then the fire of the LORD fell and burned up the sacrifice, the wood, the stones and the soil, and also licked up the water in the trench.

39 When all the people saw this, they fell prostrate and cried, "The LORD—HE IS GOD! THE LORD—HE IS GOD!"

Elijah's public prayer gives evidence of great faith and confidence that God will answer. The fire of the Lord consumes not only the burnt offering and the wood but also the inflammable stones with the water in the trenches.

The New Testament also confirms the above when Luke reports on the disciples wanting fire from heaven to destroy the Samaritans:

LUKE 9:51-56 New International Version (NIV)

51 As the time approached for him to be taken up to heaven, Jesus
resolutely set out for Jerusalem. **52** And he sent messengers on
ahead, who went into a Samaritan village to get things ready for
him; **53** but the people there did not welcome him, because he was
heading for Jerusalem. **54** When the disciples James and John saw
this, they asked, "Lord, do you want us to call fire down from heaven
to destroy them?"**55** But Jesus turned and rebuked them. **56** Then
he and his disciples went to another village.

Jesus is focused on completing his mission. This meant that he would have to make his way to Jerusalem ("*set his face to go to Jerusalem*") for his final journey to the cross. "*Taken up in heaven*" refers to Christ's ascension that awaits his final suffering, death and resurrection.

As Jesus and his disciples go south from Galilee to Jerusalem, they travel through Samaria which is traditionally known to be Samaritan territory. The reaction from the Samaritans, comes as no surprise as they did not accept Jerusalem as the place where God should be worshipped, let alone to accept any kind of offering. With this kind of expected rejection from the Samaritans we find John and James ready to avenge Jesus humiliation by calling for a fire of judgement from heaven. Jesus immediately disapproves.

From these two dramatic incidents, it seems that, in expecting God to answer prayer by means of releasing fire from heaven, was no surprise to men of God in Biblical times.

Finally, we are reminded in Luke 11:10-13, of Jesus lesson on prayer, whereby the disciples were prompted and encouraged to keep on asking for spiritual blessings (especially for the recipient of the Holy Spirit), as their heavenly Father were much better at keeping promises than their earthly fathers:

Luke 11:10-13 New International Version (NIV)

10 For everyone who asks receives; the one who seeks finds; and to the one who knocks, the door will be opened.

11 "Which of you fathers, if your son asks for a fish, will give him a
snake instead? 12 Or if he asks for an egg, will give him a scorpion? 13 If
you then, though you are evil, know how to give good gifts to your children, how much more will your Father in heaven give the Holy Spirit to those who ask him?"

Nothing has changed since the day that Jesus taught his disciples how to ask in prayer. It is still committed prayer that kindles the fire. It is still a childlike prayer filled with expectation that makes us receive the Holy Spirit to come and dwell in us.

GOD NOT ONLY WITH US BUT IN US:

When the angel Gabriel paid Mary a visit (Luke 1:26-38) in revealing God's plan to have her set apart as the mother of Jesus, it was more than just delivering a heavenly message. It was a revelation of how close God wanted to journey with us, but even more so: that God wanted to make his home within us! Mary's womb would soon become the addressee where the Saviour would reside. The New Testament teaches that as Jesus dwelled in Mary's womb, the Holy Spirit would dwell in every believer to support, strengthen and toughen us in becoming a witness of Christ. Jesus promised, in John 14:20, that the Holy Spirit would inhabit our lives when the time has come for the outpouring of the Spirit, to keep us connected and grounded in the Trinity: " On that day you will realize that I am in my Father, and you are in me, and I am in you." This is further confirmed in the writing of Paul when he declares: "...Christ lives in me" (Gal 2:20), "So that Christ may dwell in your hearts through faith" (Eph. 3:17) and "Christ is in you...the hope of glory" (Col 1:27).

Where it was the Scriptures that set the Emmaus travellers hearts' on fire in having them open their home and more importantly their life to Christ, it was now the Spirit that set the apostles' tongues on fire that would cause them to boldly share the Gospel that would eventually result in a blaze.

WHERE THE CHURCH SUBMIT TO THE ONGOING PREACHING OF CHRIST – A BLAZE IS SOON TO APPEAR

Chapter 6

THE HEAT IS ON

It is extremely dangerous when fire conditions are just about perfect during the hot dry summers in countries like the USA and Australia. Almost every year huge sections of forestry and residential areas are effected, damaged and totally destroyed because of the devastation coursed by such conditions. In most cases, it is wind gust's blowing days on end that seems to make the flames unstoppable on its course of destruction.

To create such an unstoppable blaze, you need but only a single *flame* and *wind*. In Evangelical terms, you only need the *authority of the Scriptures* and the *transformational work of the Holy Spirit* to see God create an all life-changing event. Jesus himself brought about the spark or flame that set the followers of Jesus hearts' on fire when he applied the Scriptures to himself and revealed that it was written to fulfil what was to come:

> "He said to them, 'this is what I told you while I was still with you: everything must be fulfilled that is written about me in the *Law of Moses, the Prophets and the Psalms.*'

> Then he opened their minds so they could understand the Scriptures" (Luke 24:44-45).

What is meant by *Scriptures* in the Gospel accounts?

The *Law of Moses*, הרות thorah, which includes Genesis, Exodus, Leviticus, Numbers, and Deuteronomy.

The *Prophets*, םיאיבנ , nabiaim, or teachers, includes Joshua, Judges, the two books of Samuel, and the two books of Kings: these were termed the former prophets. Isaiah, Jeremiah, Ezekiel, Hosea, Joel, Amos, Obadiah, Jonah, Micah, Nahum, Habakkuk, Zephaniah, Haggai, Zechariah, and Malachi: these were termed the latter prophets.

The *Hagiographa*, or "holy writings", םיבותכ kethuvim, which comprehended the Psalms, Proverbs, Job, Canticles, Ruth, Lamentations, Ecclesiastes, Esther, Daniel, Ezra, Nehemiah, and the two books of Chronicles. The Jews made anciently only twenty-two books of the whole, to bring them to the number of the letters in the Hebrew alphabet; and this they did by joining Ruth to Judges, making the two books of Samuel only one; and so of Kings and Chronicles; joining the Lamentations to Jeremiah, and making the twelve minor prophets only one book.

Fifty days after Jesus resurrection the transformational outpouring of the Holy Spirit took place to fuel the faith of the Apostles in helping them to finally grasp that Jesus is indeed, according to the Scriptures (Moses, the Prophets and the Psalms), the long- awaited Messiah.

This oncoming fire blaze in Acts 2 was prophesied and foretold by John the Baptist, according to the witness in Luke 3: 8-10…for it was not only to be a sign of hope to the hundred-and -twenty believers, but also a sign of judgement to those that did not heed the call to acknowledge Jesus as the Son of God:

> Produce fruit in keeping with **repentance.** And do not begin to say to yourselves, 'We have Abraham as our father.' For I tell you that out of these stones God can raise up **children** for Abraham. The axe is already at the root of

> the trees, and every tree that does not produce good fruit will be cut down and thrown into the fire.

"What should we do then?" the crowd asked.

The above section corresponds in tone and message remarkably well with Acts 2:36-40…

> Therefore, let all Israel be assured of this: God has made this Jesus, whom you crucified, both Lord and Messiah. When the people heard this, they were cut to the heart and said to Peter and the other apostles, **"Brothers, what shall we do?"**
>
> Peter replied, "**Repent** and be baptized, every one of you, in the name of Jesus Christ for the forgiveness of your sins. And you will receive the gift of the Holy Spirit. The promise is for you and your **children** and for all who are far off—for all whom the Lord our God will call.[22]

With many other words he warned them; and he pleaded with them, "Save yourselves from this corrupt generation."

According to Luke 3: 16-17 the above judgement will correspond in intensity with the devastation that is caused by fire and heat:

> John answered them all, "I baptize you with water. But one who is more powerful than I will come, the straps of whose sandals I am not worthy to untie. He will baptize you with the Holy Spirit and fire. His winnowing fork is in his hand to clear his threshing floor and to gather the

---

[22] I do not agree with some commentators using a over simplified juxtaposition which implies that *repent* aligns with *forgiveness* and (water) *baptism* with receiving the *Holy Spirit.* This is a complete denial of the context which leads us to believe that at the temple location there were not enough water to baptize 3000 people and therefore cannot imply that to receive the Holy Spirit you need to be baptized with water. Rather that it refers to the baptism of the Holy Spirit which do align well with Luke's teaching in 3:16-17.

> wheat into his barn, but he will burn up the chaff with unquenchable fire.

Jesus indeed gathered, on the day of Pentecost, wheat into his kingdom, when three thousand were added to the number of his followers (Acts 2:41).

SUBMISSION OF THE CHURCH TO THE CALL OF CHRIST:

With the outpouring of the Holy Spirit and the confusion that it brought about, an opportunity was given to the Apostles to proclaim Christ to the people, which at that time were gathered in Jerusalem for the feast of the First Fruits.[23] This was the opportunity that Jesus referred to when he instructed his followers on what will be expected from them once their hearts were set on fire and their tongues anointed from on high: *You will be my witnesses in Jerusalem…* (Acts 1:8). With the feast of the First Fruit, God had already gathered people from all different nationalities (Acts 2: 5-12) in Jerusalem. It was time to proclaim that Jesus is Lord.

Peter address the crowd in the same way that Jesus did with the Emmaus travellers:[24] He explains, according to the Jewish Scriptures, what has just happened among them in Jerusalem, by referring to the authority of the Jewish writings: The *Prophets* (Joel), the *Holy writings* (Psalms) and *Moses* (Genesis). In Peter's evangelism sermon he uses the authority of Scripture and does not rely on his own experience or witness, even in meeting with the resurrected Jesus.

He refers to the Prophet Joel 2:28-32 in Acts 2: 16-21. He refers to the book of Psalms in Psalm 16:8-11 by relating it to his sermon in Acts 2:25-28 and Psalm 110:1in Acts 2:34-35. In the actual recorded sermon or address there is no explicit reference to the *Law of Moses (The first five books of the Old Testament).* Or is there? I believe there is when Luke mentions in Acts 2:40 that Peter: "…

[23] The Feast of Pentecost or **Shavuot** has many names in the Bible: The Feast of Weeks, the Feast of Harvest, and the Latter First fruits. Celebrated on the fiftieth day after Passover, **Shavuot** is traditionally a joyous time of giving thanks and presenting offerings for the new grain of the summer wheat harvest in Israel.

[24] Luke 24:44

warned them and pleaded with them, 'Save yourself from this corrupt generation.' "I believe that Peter could have used the Genesis account of the destruction of Sodom and Gomorrah[25] according to Genesis 13:13: "Now the people of Sodom were wicked and were sinning greatly against the Lord." In Luke 10:12[26], as in other scriptural references, we find Jesus more than once referring to the devastation of Sodom when he speaks on the topic of judgement and a corrupt generation. Therefore I believe that Peter would have mentioned the history of Genesis 18-19 in his plea when addressing the people.

As Jesus exposition of the Scriptures resulted in his followers experiencing their hearts to be affected with emotion and excitement we also find the hearts' of Peters audience to experience acute and deep emotional concern and regret (Acts 2:37). Simply put they were emotionally distressed [27] (κατενυγησαν). Preaching from the Scriptures have affected Peter's audience to such an extent that they were almost desperate to find from him what they now need to do?

Now that God had blessed the preaching of Peter and the hearts of the people were touched, the spark needed fuel. Likewise, as the Holy Spirit in a physical appearance of wind introduced himself to those waiting and praying in the upper room, it was his presence needed to confirm the salvation message brought by Peter. Peter encouraged those affected to be receptive of God's gift which is the indwelling and transformational work of the Holy Spirit in each recipient's life (Acts 2:38). Once those, who took the instructions of Peter seriously, received by faith the indwelling of the Holy Spirit, the blaze swept through Jerusalem as three thousand lives were affected at once. The blaze did not stop there. According to the book of Acts the numbers grew daily as the Lord added to their number (Acts 2:47), the number of believing men grew to five thousand (Acts 4:4), more men and woman were added to the number (Acts 5:14), the number of followers was still increasing (Acts 6:1) and a large number of priests came to faith (Acts 6:7). It was indeed a sweeping blaze with devastating effects for the high priest and his associates.

---

[25] See also Genesis 18-19.

[26] See also Matthew 10:15

[27] Literally: "pierced in the heart".

What Jesus declared and longed for, according to the words spoken in Luke 12:49-53, were accomplished: From now onwards, according to the New Testament writings, people would not be primarily divided along race, colour or gender, but faith in Christ. Those who believed in Christ were called Christians[28] (Acts 11:26) and those who did not identify with such a label remained outside of the Christian circle of influence. The division that Jesus spoke of in Luke 12:51-53 were indeed now established and would be a dividing force not only among families, but also nations. A division among three global religions: Christianity, Islam and Judaism.

---

[28] Tradition holds that the first Gentile **church was** founded in Antioch, **Acts** 11:20-21, where it is recorded that the disciples of Jesus **Christ were** first **called Christians**

Chapter 7

CRITICAL REFLECTION

The critical question is asked: if the theological connection between Luke's Gospel and the book of Acts does not necessarily, by default, lie in the Gospel's post-resurrection ending, but elsewhere, is Luke 10:1-17 not the ideal section because of its clear missiological undertone? Does Luke 10:1-17 not enable a better connection with Acts 1-2, more so than Luke 12:49-53?

Luke 10:1-17 (NIV)

After this the Lord appointed seventy-two others and sent them two
by two ahead of him to every town and place where he was about
to go. 2 He told them, "The harvest is plentiful, but the workers
are few. Ask the Lord of the harvest, therefore, to send out workers
into his harvest field. 3 Go! I am sending you out like lambs among
wolves. 4 Do not take a purse or bag or sandals; and do not greet
anyone on the road.
5 "When you enter a house, first say, 'Peace to this house.' 6 If someone
who promotes peace is there, your peace will rest on them; if not, it
will return to you. 7 Stay there, eating and drinking whatever they

give you, for the worker deserves his wages. Do not move around from house to house.

8 "When you enter a town and are welcomed, eat what is offered to
you.9 Heal the sick who are there and tell them, 'The kingdom of
God has come near to you.' 10 But when you enter a town and are not
welcomed, go into its streets and say, 11 'Even the dust of your town
we wipe from our feet as a warning to you. Yet be sure of this: The
kingdom of God has come near.' 12 I tell you, it will be more bearable
on that day for Sodom than for that town.

13 "Woe to you, Chorazin! Woe to you, Bethsaida! For if the miracles
that were performed in you had been performed in Tyre and
Sidon, they would have repented long ago, sitting in sackcloth and
ashes. 14 But it will be more bearable for Tyre and Sidon at the
judgment than for you.15 And you, Capernaum, will you be lifted to
the heavens? No, you will go down to Hades

16 "Whoever listens to you listens to me; whoever rejects you rejects
me; but whoever rejects me rejects him who sent me."

17 The seventy-two returned with joy and said, "Lord, even the
demons submit to us in your name."

The above critical observation has merits for three reasons:

- The 70 names in the Genesis list (Gn.10) express the generations, of the sons of Noah, that came forth after the flood and *symbolically* express the unity of the 70 nations of the world, that were dispersed at Babel when the tower of the Babel building project came to an abrupt halt. This number (just about) correlates with Luke 10:1[29] and could reference the start of the Gospel reaching the entire world because of the outpouring of the Holy Spirit

---

[29] Many other old and reliable Greek manuscripts have 70 and interpreters agree that it is difficult to decide about which number was in the original of Luke's Gospel. As no doctrinal issue is at stake I choose to go with the number 70 for its probable symbolic significance representing the number of nations of the world (cf. Genesis 10).

on Pentecost[30], as the 72 were also sent to reach each household with the peace and blessing of the Messiah. The connection between Luke 10:1 and Acts 1-2 could therefore, be an interesting probability.

- Luke 10:2-3 reveals a connection with the command in Luke 24: 47-48 "... *and repentance for the forgiveness of sins will be preached in his name to all nations, beginning at Jerusalem. You are witnesses of these things."* Again, the interesting probability of "nations" are at play but is nevertheless a weak connection with the rest of the content in Luke chapter 10.
- Luke 24 as well as Luke 10 carries the motive of entering homes (in also gentile suburbs) in bringing the blessing of God where hospitality, in sharing in a meal, takes place. In Luke 10 it is Jesus followers that are to enter and bless the homes' of those that dwell in it. In Luke 24 it is Jesus as the risen Messiah, blessing the home of the couple travelling with Him to Emmaus, as he shares in a meal with them.

Luke 10: 1-17 cannot replace Luke 12:49-53 as a proper door hinge that opens' a gateway between Luke's Gospel on the one hand and his description on the birth and progress of the early church in the book of Acts, on the other. It becomes clear that the purpose of the seventy-two's mission was not primarily to convert households to Christ, but rather to establish a new inclusive Christ-like community by means of sharing meals together. This makes more sense if one understood the background to Jewish religious rules, especially where meals were concerned. Jews did not eat with Gentiles, as Gentiles' homes and their food were religiously unclean.

HOSPITALITY

Professor Pinchas Shir explains:[31]

[30] Acts 2:5 is of importance when it states: "Now there were dwelling in Jerusalem Jews, devout men from every nation (70) under the heaven."

[31] www.http:// Weekly. Israelbiblecenter.com

> "Jews did not eat when they visited the houses of their Gentile acquaintances, because Gentiles partook of the types of foods forbidden by Torah. Because they generally did not avoid purchasing foods already offered to Roman deities in the market. Jews had no problem eating in their own homes with Gentiles, where the commitment to purity required by Torah was guaranteed".

Thus, we find in Acts 11 that the "circumcision party" of the Christian Jews were upset with Peter – not primarily because of sharing the Gospel with Gentiles, but because he ate with them and in so doing was defiling the Jewish purity standard regulations, in bringing blemish and not blessing unto him. In some rare cases Jews did eat with Gentiles, but then they brought their own food and also ate it separately from the Gentiles. This feature is addressed in Luke 10: 4 where the seventy-two were not allowed to take money with them on their journey, as this could have made them buy their own religious food and eat it apart from the Gentiles, whom they had to reach with the hospitality of the Gospel. In the ministry of the seventy-two towards Gentiles, we find that meals that were previously understood and used as a religious ceremony that excluded others, had now become a ministry to include outsiders into the Kingdom of God. One of the most powerful instruments realising inclusivity in Luke's Gospel is table-fellowship.

Therefore, do we find, that Luke 10:1-17 does indeed have missiological motives, but focus on the importance of *hospitality* when on a mission. The connection between Luke 24 and Acts 1-2, in regards, to Luke 12:49-53 is the powerful *transformation* that takes place when we open our hearts to *Scripture – that proclaims Christ, trust in the Spirit – that transforms us to the likeness of Christ and ultimately submit ourselves – to the call of Christ.*

Chapter 8

HOW TO AWAKEN THE HEART OF YOUR CHURCH?

In this closing section, I shall try to answer the above challenging question in touching on three aspects of ministry that I call: *positioning, envisioning and acknowledging.*

POSITIONING FOR AUTHENTICITY INSTEAD OF SUCCESS:

It all starts with positioning your congregation to let go of being a success story. To not focus primarily on numbers, ratings and income, but on becoming an authentic mouthpiece for God. Authenticity is a sort after characteristic that is highly valued in Post Christendom society. In our fast track and secularised global villages, nothing seems to deliver beyond reaching its due by date label and nothing seems to excite us beyond the next buzz. True value, is among other criteria, appreciated for not only its longevity but its authenticity. Being authentic means coming from a real place within. It is when our actions and words are congruent with our believes and values. It is being ourselves, not an imitation of what we think we should be or have been told to be.

Postmodern people are seeking for such authentic personal encounters, genuine experience without simply following those who claim to have it. Those days are long gone. If what the Church preach and proclaim is only to excite and boost its numbers or not be attainable by the least among us…it is not the gospel. For the Gospel of Jesus Christ speaks of a genuine God who genuinely answers those who call, seek and knock.

Luke explains brilliantly to his readers in the book of Acts, that the birth and growth of the first congregation after Pentecost and its ongoing blaze was not based on human engineering, but on Godly initiative. Therefore the birth and expansion of the congregation in Jerusalem are to be interpreted and understood as authentic because the congregation in Jerusalem never intended to grow beyond its Jewish borderlines. Even in spite of clear commissioning to evangelise (Acts 1:8). It becomes clear that those first believers were finding it hard to play catch-up with God. Those early days in the ministry of the Apostles are a testimony of them mainly seeing God at work. What were they then doing? Trying to catch up with the ever- spreading blaze that started on Pentecost.

THE CHURCH IN ACTS: AN EVER CATHING-UP-WITH-GOD KIND OF CHURCH

In Acts 1:12-26 we find the apostles chose Matthias to replace Judas who betrayed Jesus. Why was it important for the apostles to be restored back to the number twelve? Was this because Matthias was such an extraordinary and charismatic witness? No. It was because of a Jewish conviction that being twelve apostles are to be representative of the twelve tribes of Israel. It was due to a deep-rooted conviction that God is primarily concerned for the salvation of Israel. At its worse, it was a clear motive to preserve and protect the new religious movement from becoming less Jewish and more Gentile to their liking. Very soon in the Acts account, even amidst the excitement of the Holy Spirit moving like a blaze, it becomes clear that the apostles had their own agenda and would not in themselves adhere to the commissioning of Acts 1:8 to become witnesses outside of their beloved Jewish city-Jerusalem.

This becomes evident when we read in Acts 2:46 and 3:1 that the Apostles would go up to the temple for the different Jewish times of prayer. The Temple was the pinnacle of being committed to the Jewish lifestyle and for protecting Jewish culture and tradition against the worldly spirit of the Gentiles. But this was soon to change.

The Holy Spirit, in wanting to direct its blaze further from Jerusalem to the ends of the earth had to deal with the Apostles and the early church in a firm way that would help them understand the urgency of moving with the Spirit and not against it. Therefore do we see in Acts 8:1 that God allows for great persecution to break out against the church in Jerusalem and have believers scattered throughout Judea and Samaria so that those believers and witnesses could keep up with the spread of the powerful impact of the Holy Spirit. It is a stark reminder that if the Church does not move with the authentic plan of God (Acts 1:8), but sets its own agenda then she set her up for hardship (Acts 8:1).

If the first congregation was to be used by the Holy Spirit to also reach the Gentiles in a genuine and authentic way, then there was a lot of catching up for the church to do. Jewish folk would not mingle or eat with Gentiles under normal circumstances. But this was to be challenged.

In Acts 10 we read of the Holy Spirit blaze powerfully reaching the Gentiles and therefore for a second "Pentecost" event to occur in Acts 10:45. This time the recipients were Gentiles and not Jews. "The circumcised (Jewish) believers who had come with Peter were astonished that the gift of the Holy Spirit had been poured out even on Gentiles." What made this event occur and what made Peter to at last catch up with the blaze of the Spirit reaching these Gentiles? According to Acts 10:9-48 we find Peter spending time in prayer with God as he fell into a trance where he saw heaven open with a large sheet being let down to earth. It contained all kinds of four-footed animals, as well as reptiles and birds. Then Peter heard a voice tell him: "Get up, Peter. Kill and eat" (Acts 10:13). Peter refused in hearing this command for it would not only be a violation of Jewish food laws, but he would become ritually unclean as well. God would soon reveal to Peter that He was overturning the Jewish dietary laws in general so that nothing would get in the way of fellowship with Gentiles. Then Peter began to speak: " I now realize how true it is that God does not show favouritism but accepts from every nation the one who fears him and does what is right" (Acts 10:34-35).

If our churches are not positioned and committed to keeping up with God's authentic strategy of *proclaiming Christ* and in so doing be *transformed to the likeness of Christ,* we shall not only fall short of *submission to the call of Christ* but mistakenly confuse momentarily success with the blessing of God. I rather am part of a catching-up-with-God kind of church and lack behind other so-called successful churches; than to find myself reaching the top of the ladder only to find that it is facing the wrong way! Let the Holy Spirit lead the way, not the success manual.

ENVISIONING CREATIVITY AND INNOVATION - NOT STAGNATION:

The early church was given the Holy Spirit on the day of Pentecost to become one of the greatest movements of all time. The apostles with their followers were set up to become a force that was to influence the community of their day. From the Gospel writings, it appears that Jesus had no intention of founding a new local religious order as his followers were not given any creed, rite or geographical centre from which to operate. Rather they received a universal mandate to share their new found freedom, from sin and guilt, in the risen Lord, with all of humanity and never to protect themselves from the consequences of it.

David Bosch[32] (1993:50) reminds us that: "This high level of calling was, however, not maintained for long. Their survival as a separate religious group, rather than their commitment to the reign of God, began to preoccupy them. It ceased to be a movement and turned into an institution." This tendency, in early Christianity, to not remain a movement appeared to be irreversible as bishops (or elders) and deacons settled in their ministry toward becoming an

[32] David J. Bosch, *Transforming Mission* (Maryknoll, New York: Orbis Books, 1993), 50.

institution. As time went by the struggle for survival as a separate religious establishment consumed Christians energy. Sociological law predicts that any given movement in due time either disintegrates or becomes institutionalised. The same was bound to happen to the early Christian movement. It could not, in the long run, survive merely in the shape of a charismatic leader with his band of lower-class artisans from the periphery of society. Something had to change.

BEAUTY:

An important question that I was confronted with in ministry in my own century old institution was **what kind of exciting and future potential our church have or aspire to that can contribute towards enhancing our worship in a Post Christendom culture? How can we keep the fire and momentum going in spite of stagnation that sets in after some time?** In knowing that in our, predominantly, Post-Christian society there is the tendency and need to deconstruct sermons and teachings to be able to critically respond to what is presented during worship, we wanted to establish a place where such *critical openness* could be adhered to as an extension of the formal worship service.

The expectation was that St. Andrews Sunday morning worship service, would continue after the blessing was said in a space that was welcoming and hospitable for anyone to contribute to what they have heard during the formal service. This had to be a space that was warm, inviting and beautifully set so that anyone could have a coffee or tea and feel inspired to start a conversation with someone else in regards to the message that they have just heard in the pews.

Worship, in whatever form it is presented in or service it renders, is not intended to last only for an hour on a Sunday. It is intended to carry us into the next week and to give us a focal point to focus our discipleship on as we prepare for our next meeting. It is supposed to be carried into our homes and the work place, but then freely chosen as an extension of the formal worship as depicted in Deuteronomy 6:6-9

> 6 "These commandments that I give you today are to be on your hearts.7 Impress them on your children. Talk about

> them when you sit at home and when you walk along the road, when you lie down and when you get up. [8] Tie them as symbols on your hands and bind them on your foreheads. Write them on the door frames of your houses and on your gates."

This was indeed my vision when I explored what options our little church property could render us as far as "door frames" and "gates" could allow us! We needed a space that we could decorate and infuse with beauty that would carry worshippers from the pews into the continuous presence of God where their conversations and fellowship would simply be an extension of where they have just come from and where they would be of too soon.

St. Andrews is small and its building leaves us with limitations. But we had a small lounge area directly from the worship area. We started stripping it away. Clearing it from its past, but at the same time infusing it with all kinds of new possibilities. We made it into a stylish coffee shop and lounge with self-serving coffee and tea urns for hospitality, small tables to establish intimacy in conversations and even a small library corner with a room where people can pray for one another.

It is our prayer that this lounge will be a space where the sermon will resonate for some time longer in the memory of those that have just heard it. Space where it will be safe to discuss the message and to openly and critically reflect on it as more investigation and conversation occurs. Space where some may find acceptance and others forgiveness. Space where members and visitors alike can journey from the *place of God* (formal worship area) to the *face of God* (this beautiful space where informal worship continuous as individuals come to appreciate their significant other)…a place, just short of the Holy of Holies!

The result of creating such a place of beauty and hospitality is that we have created a space where *critical openness* can take place. People have the opportunity to engage with what they have heard and experienced during worship on an empirical level and work it out for themselves in a safe and secure surrounding.

ACKNOWLEDGE PEOPLE – NOT PROGRAMMES:

In the last quarter of the twentieth century political, sexual, social and artistic ideologies began to be questioned, particularly the Modernism faith in the benefits of scientific progress and mass culture. This led to a series of shifts in Western philosophical thinking that came to be defined as Post-Modernism.[33]

Post-Modernism is, in essence, an individualist philosophy. Individualists encourage the exercise of an individual's human - and political rights and therefore value independence and self-reliance. They also argue that the interests of the individual are more important than those of the state or of any social group. They, therefore, oppose external interference by society or the government on the interests of the individual. The extreme results of this is an increase in conspiracy theories in regards to world governments where the individual is at risk.

During the last quarter of the twentieth century, Post-Modernist and individualist thinking had a profound impact on people who often had never heard of the terms or, if they had, could not define them. There was a growing reluctance to make a commitment to organisations and movements which might get in the way of the priorities of the individual:

- Membership of mainstream political parties fell sharply
    - At the same time, the number of uncommitted voters, whose allegiance fluctuated from one election to another according to their individual preferences, grew.
- Mainstream religious observance declined
    - For people of faith, allegiance to traditional Christian denominations became looser, as believers sought out groups who provided the best fit with their own individual beliefs
    - Others favoured exploring their own interpretation of 'spirituality' as opposed to accepting the truth claims of orthodox religion.

---

[33] www.https//:crossref – it.info

INDIVIDUALITY:

Although such a drastic Post Christendom paradigm shift has left the Church bewildered, damaged and its future uncertain we in the field of missiology believe that this kind of change is to be regarded as not the end of religion, but a new opportunity for the Church to re-establish its core business in a contemporary fashion.

In the context mentioned above, it is striking that Luke comments specifically that: "They saw what seemed to be tongues of fire that separated and came to rest on each (*one* = *ενα*) of them" (Acts 2:3). Each individual that was in the upper room at the time that the Holy Spirit was released, received the gift of the Spirit in his and her own right. Although the promise of the Holy Spirit was a collective blessing intended for the Church as the body of Christ, it nevertheless was intended to equip and empower each individual for his or her own Christian journey towards maturity.

I am not promoting consumerism and individuality in our churches where serving the needs of the individual now becomes the latest criteria for congregational leadership. I do however promote an evangelical mature like spirituality where believers are encouraged to know the leading and guidance of the Holy Spirit in a personal way that enables one to understand the presence and power of the risen Lord in one's own walk.

Our churches lack maturity in regards to three concurrent issues. The first concerns pastors being overworked with symptoms of burn-out due to members exclusively consulting their church leadership without acknowledging the direct input and leading of the Word and Spirit. The more members understand the person and purpose of the Holy Spirit in their own lives the more they are prone to consult with God through personal devotions and prayer than solely relying on congregational leaders and initiatives.

The second issue is somewhat the reverse where church members are prone to be caught up in the damaging consequences of spiritual abuse. This is the scenario where church pastors and associates practice their own right to control their members by enforcing or withholding information that makes them dependant on their leadership and not independent mature Christians. Preaching and teaching only specific scriptures that enforce the leaders' religious ideology, applying scripture out of context and manipulating doctrine to such an extent that a sectarian environment is established.

Where an independent attitude co-exists among members to at least investigate the Scriptures for themselves and not to exclusively rely on the teaching of the clergy, we find not only a greater mature following but also an understanding of the Reformed teaching encouraging the *Priesthood of all believers.*

Third and finally it is meaningful that the author of the Gospel of Luke mentions that the Spirit was given to each one in the upper room as proof that God not only loves and care for his Church collectively but also in an intimate personal way. The Spirit support us and guide us, to know Christ in a most personal and individual way, no matter what season of life we are in:

"'In the last days, God says,
I will pour out my Spirit on all people.
Your **sons** and **daughters** will prophesy,
your **young men** will see visions,
your **old men** will dream dreams.
18 Even on my **servants**, both **men** and **women,**
I will pour out my Spirit in those days,
and they will prophesy'"[34]

---

[34] NIV Acts 2:17-18

Chapter 9

YOUR LOCAL CHURCH IS GOD'S NEW CREATION

Can the heart of the Church be resuscitated? Can the Church be awakened to a new way of ministry and service to God and the world? Yes! I do believe that the abundant and powerful life of the Church portrait in Acts 2:42-47 is not only attainable but also maintainable, because ***the local church does have the capacity to transform its ministries and survive any transitional season for it has the capacity to flourish in its core DNA.***[35]

To understand the depth of the question: *Why is this going on?* We have to start at the beginning of creation as it is described in the book of Genesis. The Garden of Eden represents a place of belonging for mankind. First God created a world (habitat) for us to belong to (Gen.1:1). Secondly, God created the Garden of Eden for Adam to *purposefully attend to work* and in so doing find a place of belonging where he could live and work with purpose (Gen.2:15/19). Finally,

---

[35] Mario Weyers, *Your church is God's new creation.* (New-Delhi: Christian World Imprints, 2018), 33.

God created Eve for Adam so that mankind can also belong with one another (Gen.2:18-25).

Apart from these macro themes we also find God creating four essentials to this life:

- Beauty
- Prosperity
- Purpose
- Community

We start with *beauty* (Gen.2:8-9):

> Now the LORD God had planted a garden in the east, in Eden; and there he put the man he had formed. The Lord God made all kinds of trees grow out of the ground—trees that were pleasing to the eye and good for food. In the middle of the garden were the tree of life and the tree of the knowledge of good and evil.

The trees were "pleasing to the eye" which means that the concept of beauty was introduced in God's act of creation.

God also created *prosperity* (Gen.2:10-12):

> A river watering the garden flowed from Eden; from there it was separated into four headwaters. The name of the first is the Pishon, it winds through the entire land of Havilah, where there is gold. (The gold of that land is good; aromatic resin and onyx are also there).

Gold and gems were introduced in the creation process which makes God, and not a man, the author of prosperity.

God gave Adam the task of caring for what He had created, for what He placed in nature and for managing creation's natural and rich resources. Thus giving *purpose* to Adam's life (Gen.2:19-20):

> Now the LORD God had formed out of the ground all the wild animals and all the birds in the sky. He brought them to the man to see what he would name them; and whatever the man called each living creature, that was its name. So

> the man gave names to all the livestock, the birds in the sky and all the wild animals.36

God created purpose and therefore the possibility to live a meaningful and purpose-filled life.

Finally and most profoundly, God created a *community* (Gen.2:21-22):

> The LORD God caused the man to fall into a deep sleep; and while he was sleeping, he took one of the man's ribs and then closed up the place with flesh. Then the Lord God made a woman from the rib he had taken out of the man, and he brought her to the man.

Adam at last, had company that was not from the animal kingdom, but one of his own kind. In joining Adam and Eve together God introduced community in its simplest and basic form.

In Genesis 3 we read of the disobedience of man and the consequence of taking matters in one's own hands. Once Adam and Eve had eaten from the tree of knowledge of good and evil they realised that they were naked (Gen.3:7). Curse instead of blessing came into being. What once was beautiful to Adam and Eve in regards to God's creation ("that was pleasing to the eye") has now turned to embarrassment:

> But the LORD God called to the man, 'Where are you?' He answered, 'I heard you in the garden, and I was afraid because I was naked; so I hid.' And he said, 'Who told you that you were naked? Have you eaten from the tree that I commanded you not to eat from? (Gen.3:9-11).

Where Adam and Eve had the privilege of sharing in the abundance and prosperity of the fruit coming from the trees that they were allowed to eat, they now had to work hard producing their own food from the land that was cursed:

---

[36] Gen.1:26 " Then God said: ' "Let us make mankind in our image, in our likeness, so that they may rule over The fish in the sea and the birds in the sky, over the livestock and all the wild animals, and over all the Creatures that move along the ground.'"

> Cursed is the ground because of you; through painful toil you will eat food from it all the days of your life. It will produce thorns and thistles for you, and you will eat the plants of the field (Gen.3:17-18).

Furthermore, they lost their sense of purposeful living and working for a bigger course than just surviving and "paying the bills every month".

> By the sweat of your brow you will eat your food until you return to the ground (Gen.3:19).

It was no longer a situation where Adam and Eve were engaging with occupational activities because it gave purpose to their lives, but now they had to work in order to eat and finally to stay alive. The creational side of daily activities had to make way for the necessity of labour for without it they would die.

Finally, the sense of community between man and woman were badly effected as Adam blamed Eve for their kingdom lost and Eve on her turn put the blame on the snake (Evil):

> "The man said, 'The woman you put here with me—she gave me some fruit from the tree, and I ate it.'" "Then the LORD God said to the woman, 'What is this you have done?' " "The woman said, 'The serpent deceived me, and I ate'" (Gen.3:12-13).

These unfortunate turn of events teaches us that mankind lost its place of belonging due to the introduction of sin into creation (Gen.3). Man's relationship with God, the cosmos and with his fellow man was badly affected. (Gen.3:23). "So the LORD God banished him from the Garden of Eden to work the ground from which he had been taken."

The Genesis account confronts us to acknowledge that in our churches and in our communities (as in our own personal makeup) we struggle to see the *beauty* of individuals that we live and work with. We tend to focus on people's mistakes and shortcomings and fail therefore to appreciate the significant other. Many church meetings and their agendas are filled with crisis management issues and business-like decisions to be made that hardly ever deals with appreciating what we have and what God has entrusted to our care. *Prosperity* has wrongly become connected with the offering and collections our church manage in a given financial year and not always expressed that it is the blessing of the Lord's involvement and care on our projects and products that makes us rich and prosperous. For many youngsters in society, prosperity is mainly measured in quantity and less in quality. For others that have already advanced in life, living a comfortable (financial) lifestyle by the age of retirement is what makes one be seen as successful. *Purpose* is a topic that is not easily associated with ones calling or "higher purpose" as there are no more grand stories that explain reality. My purpose, therefore, is no longer something I need to discover from a Father God that has purposefully "created" me, (Psalm 139) as I now create it myself according to my own believes and expectations. *Community* and a sense of belonging with others seem to be easy to find but hard to maintain as we deal with different personalities, generational struggles and conflict in our churches and in our communities. Stephen Hill (2017:403) rightly says:

> Since the great disruption of the fall, humanity has been orphaned. We feel lost and alone in the world. Without the love of the Father at the deep essential core of our being, we are abandoned and utterly alone, disconnected and confused, without direction in this life. There is an existential homelessness at the core of our humanity.[37]

WHAT OUGHT TO BE GOING ON?

In the New Testament with the coming and outpouring of the Holy Spirit, the Church is birthed as the *new* creation of God. Since its birth on the day of Pentecost, the Church is God's instrument to help us regain our sense of belonging with God and one another. The following is an indication of what ought to be going on in our congregations:

---

[37] Stephen Hill, *John-A Prophetic Revelation* (USA/NZ: Stephen Hill Publishers, 2017).

Beauty was restored with the establishment of the first Christian community: "*Everyone was filled with awe at the many wonders and signs performed by the apostles*" (Acts 2:43). Just as God's creating power was appealing to the first human's eyes in the Garden of Eden so were the new believers amazed at what they witnessed with their own eyes-the *powerful* work of God in restoring health and life in a supernatural manner. God's powerful work was truly amazing and witnessing it with their own eyes was a confirmation to their faith.

Secondly, we see from Acts chapter 2 that *prosperity* was restored in the Church: "*They sold property and possessions to give to anyone who had need*" (Acts 2:45). There was no lack of resources as the early believers' shared material life in all its facets with one another.

Purpose followed as we read in the following verses: "*They devoted themselves to the apostles' teaching and to fellowship, to the breaking of bread and to prayer. Every day they continued to meet together in the temple courts*" (Acts 2:42/47). To worship God and serve their fellow man daily, became their highest calling and sense of living purposefully.

Finally the *community* came to the forefront in Acts 2:44. "*All the believers were together and had everything in common.*" Sharing among one another and caring for one another became the rule of thumb by which the early Christians established their fellowship.

What does this reveal? *The Church is God's new creation where mankind can regain the capacity of belonging to God and regain fellowship with others.* God is one of restoration. He not only restores us back to a living relationship with Him but restores beauty back into our acts of worship. In meeting the needs of others we see God bringing partnerships into being. As we grow into more obedient Disciples of Christ and encourage each other in the ministry of discipleship we regain our true sense of calling and purpose. We start to appreciate fellowship with one another and with those in our community. We ourselves become a new creation! That is what ought to be going on!

APPENDIX

The fire prayer[38]

Holy Spirit, set me on fire with your wisdom,
so that I may love only that which is holy.

Holy Spirit, enlighten me with your understanding,
so that I may perceive only that which is holy.

Holy Spirit, kindle in me your counsel,
so that I may see only that which is holy.

Holy Spirit, inflame me with your strength,
so that I may desire only that which is holy.

Holy Spirit, pour out your knowledge upon me,
so that I may do only that which is holy.

Holy Spirit, give me ardent devotion,
so that I may seek only that which is holy.

Holy Spirit, make me blaze in the fear of God
so that I may never again lose that which is holy.

---

[38] From the Book of Devotions – Devocionário – of the Franciscan Congregation of Nursing Sisters of the Immaculate Conception, Portugal.

BIBLIOGRAPHY

Abbott, Kirsten. "Themes in Luke's Gospel: Introduction to the Luke/Acts package". www.http://wn.anglican.org.nz/resources/links/teaching_helpful_links. 2015.

Bosch, David. *Transforming Mission.* Maryknoll, New York: Orbis Books, 1993.

Hill, Stephen. *John-A Prophetic Revelation.* USA/NZ: Stephen Hill Publishers, 2017.

Horton, Michael. *For Calvinism.* Grand Rapids, Michigan: Zondervan, 2011.

Missler, Chuck. *Learn the Bible in 24 Hours.* Nashville: Thomas Nelson, 2002.

Roland, Allen. *Missionary Methods: St. Pauls or Ours?* London: Dominion Press, 1962.

Shir, Pinchas. "To eat or not to eat." Israel Bible Weekly. www.http://Israelbiblecenter.com

Feb. 28, 2017.

Soal Alexander and Henry Desmond. The Reversal of Babel: Questioning the early Church's understanding of the gift of the Holy Spirit in Acts as a reversal of the curse of Babel. *Verbum et Ecclesia, vol. 39, no.1 (2018).*

Thomas R. Schreiner, ed., *ESV Study Bible: Luke.* Wheaton: Crossway, 2008.

Weyers, Mario. *From Minutes that Matter to Sermons that Surprise.* New Delhi: Christian World Imprints, 2019.

Weyers, Mario. *Your Church is God's New Creation*. New Delhi: Christian World Imprints, 2018.